ACTIVITY PUZZLE BOOK

FOR KIDS

Belongs to:

_____

To solve this book you will need:
pencil, eraser and colouring
pencils

The aim of activity games such as word search, crosswords, dot to dot, coloring by numbers, word scramble, are fantastic for learning at any age but are particularly important for young children. Research has shown that games are essential for healthy development in early childhood and beyond.

WORD SEARCH

OCEAN LIFE

Can you find all the hidden words
in the puzzle below?

```
N W S E S I T A S N
Y L H H B M U L T H
T Z B A I D R G A O
C R A B L P T A R K
S N U I S E L E F C
S H E L L Q E G I O
S H A R K X U G S R
D O L P H I N I H A
S E A G U L L G D L
T Q S Q T O V V Z S
```

ALGAE
CORAL
CRAB
DOLPHIN
SEAGULL
SHARK

SHELL
SHIP
SQUID
STARFISH
TURTLE
WHALE

THE SPACE

Can you find all the hidden words
in the puzzle below?

```
K  S  U  Q  D  F  A  M  Y  P
Y  A  G  E  E  Q  S  E  X  L
R  T  R  J  H  S  T  T  V  A
O  E  A  D  D  H  R  E  E  N
C  L  V  S  M  U  O  O  N  E
K  L  I  T  O  T  N  R  U  T
E  I  T  A  O  T  A  I  S  S
T  T  Y  R  N  L  U  T  Z  H
Z  E  S  U  N  E  T  E  N  N
T  E  L  E  S  C  O  P  E  T
```

ASTRONAUT
GRAVITY
METEORITE
MOON
PLANETS
ROCKET

SATELLITE
SHUTTLE
STAR
SUN
TELESCOPE
VENUS

SPORTS

Can you find all the hidden words
in the puzzle below?

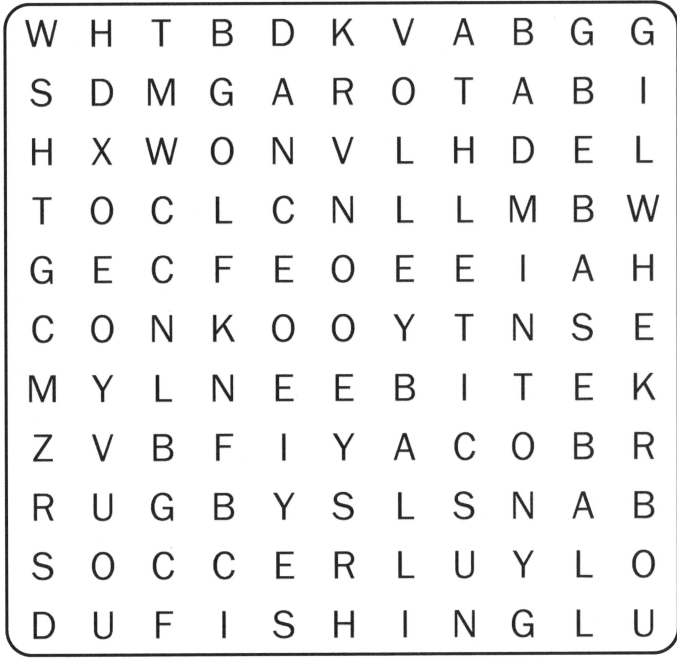

W H T B D K V A B G G
S D M G A R O T A B I
H X W O N V L H D E L
T O C L C N L L M B W
G E C F E O E E I A H
C O N K O O Y T N S E
M Y L N E E B I T E K
Z V B F I Y A C O B R
R U G B Y S L S N A B
S O C C E R L U Y L O
D U F I S H I N G L U

ATHLETICS
BADMINTON
BASEBALL
DANCE
FISHING
GOLF

GOLF
HOCKEY
RUGBY
SOCCER
TENNIS
VOLLEYBALL

THE JUNGLE

Can you find all the hidden words
in the puzzle below?

```
Z  E  B  R  A  L  C  I  C  G  T
E  L  E  P  H  A  N  T  H  I  I
N  Q  J  H  I  P  P  O  A  R  G
I  N  T  A  B  B  O  O  M  A  E
P  Y  O  P  G  T  X  U  E  F  R
A  F  U  S  I  U  K  F  L  F  H
R  B  C  N  H  J  A  R  E  E  U
R  F  A  A  O  T  W  R  O  G  W
O  M  N  K  O  Y  O  Y  N  M  K
T  N  W  E  I  N  S  E  C  T  S
X  F  H  M  O  N  K  E  Y  S  N
```

CHAMELEON
ELEPHANT
GIRAFFE
HIPPO
INSECTS
JAGUAR

MONKEY
PARROT
SNAKE
TIGER
TOUCAN
ZEBRA

THE FARM

Can you find all the hidden words
in the puzzle below?

S	V	F	J	T	G	S	V	C	J	T
H	W	W	J	O	O	C	C	N	O	V
E	T	P	Y	C	O	A	H	D	W	W
E	E	W	I	L	S	R	F	E	R	D
P	G	A	Q	G	E	E	I	E	N	I
X	G	F	M	U	C	C	U	O	E	M
R	S	H	A	H	O	R	C	W	M	D
C	O	R	N	R	W	O	O	O	F	Q
K	Q	F	N	M	M	W	B	A	R	N
D	O	N	K	E	Y	E	P	R	F	S
D	C	J	C	M	A	V	R	K	B	H

BARN
CORN
COW
DONKEY
EGGS
FARMER

FEED
GOOSE
HEN
PIG
SCARECROW
SHEEP

SHAPES

Can you find all the hidden words
in the puzzle below?

T	R	I	A	N	G	L	E	J	R	K
H	J	R	H	O	M	B	U	S	E	P
T	E	Q	C	S	S	C	R	H	C	E
C	R	A	K	X	Q	O	N	U	T	N
W	I	G	R	X	U	N	W	H	A	T
O	T	R	A	T	A	E	G	H	N	A
Z	V	Y	C	Z	R	Y	E	B	G	G
A	T	A	O	L	E	C	Z	D	L	O
D	M	M	L	Y	E	F	U	V	E	N
N	P	Y	R	A	M	I	D	B	V	Q
A	S	T	A	R	V	I	M	R	E	Y

CIRCLE
CONE
CUBE
HEART
OVAL
PENTAGON

PYRAMID
RECTANGLE
RHOMBUS
SQUARE
STAR
TRIANGLE

BIRTHDAY

Can you find all the hidden words
in the puzzle below?

```
G V V W C G I F T S F
A U I I A F O G R B A
M Q E S N M U D F A M
E E H H D D G N R L I
S M V E L N K S I L L
M Y U S E D K L E O Y
C Q S S S L Z Y N N Y
X A D E I X P Z D S N
X H K B Z C B G S Y J
H X M E C A N D I E S
S U R P R I S E L F J
```

BALLONS
CAKE
CANDIES
CANDLES
FAMILY
FRIENDS

FUN
GAMES
GIFTS
MUSIC
SURPRISE
WISHES

AT THE BEACH

Can you find all the hidden words
in the puzzle below?

```
F L I P F L O P S H C
B U C K E T X K E E A
S U N G L A S S E S S
S A N D W I Y U I T T
S H E L L C K M J R L
R O J Z P E I B V O E
U M K D S C T R P P P
W A V E S R E E M I Q
A K O D J E D L U C I
P F J X M A B L I A F
R E L A X M N A Y L E
```

BUCKET
CASTLE
FLIP FLOPS
ICE CREAM
KITE
RELAX

SAND
SHELL
SUNGLASSES
TROPICAL
UMBRELLA
WAVES

HALLOWEEN

Can you find all the hidden words
in the puzzle below?

P	S	H	O	Z	M	W	I	D	W	S
U	C	O	C	S	O	E	J	N	I	K
M	A	C	T	T	J	M	Q	H	T	E
P	R	R	O	D	R	X	B	Z	C	L
K	Y	P	B	P	R	E	T	I	H	E
I	C	A	E	S	Q	A	A	E	E	T
N	G	P	R	D	P	Y	C	T	Q	O
G	H	O	S	T	S	I	G	U	S	N
V	A	M	P	I	R	E	D	R	L	A
M	O	N	S	T	E	R	S	E	S	A
S	C	W	A	K	A	R	S	I	R	V

DRACULA
GHOSTS
MONSTERS
OCTOBER
PUMPKIN
SCARY

SKELETON
SPIDER
TREATS
VAMPIRE
WITCH
ZOMBIE

CHRISTMAS

Can you find all the hidden words
in the puzzle below?

```
D S S T O C K I N G I X
S A N T A C L A U S D
C M I D Z K E L F N S
T O Q M Y S N O W Q D
S O O R E I N D E E R
P I Y K S I Y Q R H W
X T G S I L T M S P R
G X Z H R E E F L I E
F R O S T Y S I Y C A
P R E S E N T G G N T
P S N O W M A N Z H H
```

COOKIES
ELF
FROSTY
PRESENT
REINDEER
SANTA CLAUS

SLEIGH
SNOW
SNOWMAN
STOCKING
TOYS
WREATH

VEHICLES

Can you find all the hidden words
in the puzzle below?

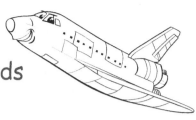

S	S	D	V	S	F	P	M	H	S	T
M	U	K	S	H	Z	T	L	H	F	A
O	T	B	H	I	U	L	R	A	K	X
O	T	T	R	J	M	P	X	U	B	A	N	I
O	U	Y	X	A	T	R	A	M	I	E
R	C	C	G	F	R	H	R	W	Q	N
C	K	B	D	E	G	I	M	I	I	M
Y	I	A	U	T	X	G	N	E	F	S
C	C	R	S	S	G	S	I	E	O	E
L	A	S	S	G	F	E	R	R	Y	N
E	R	S	C	O	O	T	E	R	V	B

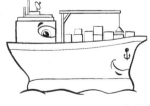

BUS
CAR
FERRY
MOTORCYCLE
PLANE
SCOOTER

SHIP
SUBMARINE
TAXI
TRAIN
TRAM
TRUCK

FRUITS

Can you find all the hidden words
in the puzzle below?

F L W L X Z W S M A F
O R A N G E A T A P Y
I P M W K A T R N R P
C G E Z G P E A G I E
H R R A D P R W O C A
E A I C R L M B I O C
R P T N H E E E D T H
R E T B V T L R E Z G
Y C W S Q N O R B Z U
I X K I W I N Y A X D
P I N E A P P L E Y O

APPLE
APRICOT
CHERRY
GRAPE
KIWI
MANGO

ORANGE
PEACH
PEAR
PINEAPPLE
STRAWBERRY
WATERMELON

VEGETABLES

Can you find all the hidden words
in the puzzle below?

P	E	P	P	E	R	S	C	C	E	O
C	A	B	B	A	G	E	O	E	G	N
C	J	S	H	B	B	J	R	L	G	I
L	E	T	T	U	C	E	N	E	P	O
V	Y	T	J	Y	P	M	P	R	L	N
S	Q	L	U	B	W	E	A	Y	A	S
C	A	R	R	O	T	S	A	A	N	T
Z	U	C	C	H	I	N	I	S	T	V
P	O	T	A	T	O	E	S	V	I	Q
J	C	L	L	C	O	V	B	D	G	O
T	O	M	A	T	O	E	S	E	J	G

CABBAGE
CARROTS
CELERY
CORN
EGGPLANT
LETTUCE

ONIONS
PEAS
PEPPERS
POTATOES
TOMATOES
ZUCCHINI

FALL

Can you find all the hidden words
in the puzzle below?

H L V A C O R N S H F
S A E Y E L L O W A Z
U S R A A X M M S L C
N V E V V A R U Q L A
F S D A E E K S U O P
L B L A S S S H I W P
O R S I O O T R R E L
W U A K C D N O R E E
E Q Z I E C D O E N P
R T O X N R A M L Y I
S O R A N G E S S J E

ACORNS
APPLE PIE
HALLOWEEN
HARVEST
LEAVES
MUSHROOMS

ORANGE
RAIN
SEASON
SQUIRRELS
SUNFLOWERS
YELLOW

SPRING

Can you find all the hidden words
in the puzzle below?

```
R M C H H L R K R R P
A N M G B I R D S A Q
I E E J J G Y Y A B H
N X G S Y A F L R B B
B J L R T I B A F I T
O Q N B E L O D G T U
W S B C Q E K Y A S L
P I C N I C N B R B I
M A Y A F E N U D E P
U W Y F W E I G E E S
F L O W E R S S N L K
```

BEE
BIRDS
FLOWERS
GARDEN
GREEN
LADYBUGS

MAY
NEST
PICNIC
RABBITS
RAINBOW
TULIPS

JOBS

Can you find all the hidden words
in the puzzle below?

D	E	N	T	I	S	T	O	L	Z	T
P	E	P	Z	C	H	P	B	A	Z	E
I	N	O	D	C	H	M	W	W	C	A
L	G	L	R	A	D	E	K	Y	Q	C
O	I	I	I	R	W	O	F	E	H	H
T	N	C	V	P	N	A	C	R	D	E
N	E	E	E	E	F	U	I	T	D	R
L	E	M	R	N	I	Q	R	T	O	R
X	R	A	J	T	F	L	X	S	E	R
M	O	N	B	E	Z	H	D	T	E	R
H	M	P	V	R	Q	Q	K	X	N	F

CARPENTER
CHEF
DENTIST
DOCTOR
DRIVER
ENGINEER

LAWYER
NURSE
PILOT
POLICEMAN
TEACHER
WAITER

SCIENCE

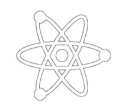

Can you find all the hidden words
in the puzzle below?

```
M P N E C A Y Q M L E
A A A L N E T D P A X
G Z T C R E L O V B P
N H U F R K R L M O E
E G R X Z I B G G R R
T D E V I R U S Y A I
O R G A N I S M O T M
B A C T E R I A Y O E
P A K O J I V X V R N
C H E M I S T R Y Y T
M I C R O S C O P E E
```

ATOM
BACTERIA
CELL
CHEMISTRY
ENERGY
EXPERIMENT

LABORATORY
MAGNET
MICROSCOPE
NATURE
ORGANISM
VIRUS

MYTHICAL BEASTS

Can you find all the hidden words
in the puzzle below?

```
U  J  M  M  D  N  W  G  D  O  O
F  F  C  I  R  O  T  O  D  P  H
A  S  C  N  R  S  D  B  R  V  C
I  G  V  O  Y  Z  P  L  A  O  Y
R  N  Y  T  M  E  B  I  G  F  C
Y  O  N  A  N  S  T  N  O  T  L
O  M  V  U  S  X  I  I  N  R  O
A  E  A  R  F  A  U  N  F  O  P
P  H  O  E  N  I  X  X  U  L  S
U  N  I  C  O  R  N  D  Z  L  N
P  U  L  A  M  E  R  M  A  I  D
```

CYCLOPS
DRAGON
FAIRY
FAUN
GNOME
GOBLIN

MERMAID
MINOTAUR
PHOENIX
TROLL
UNICORN
YETI

MAZES

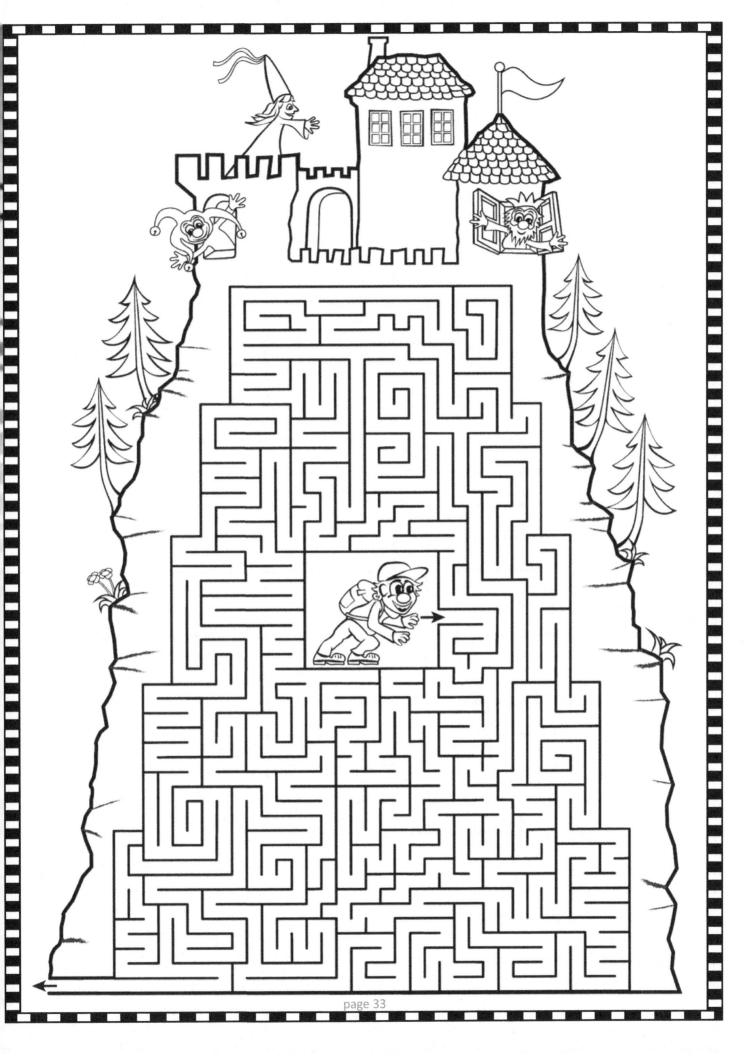

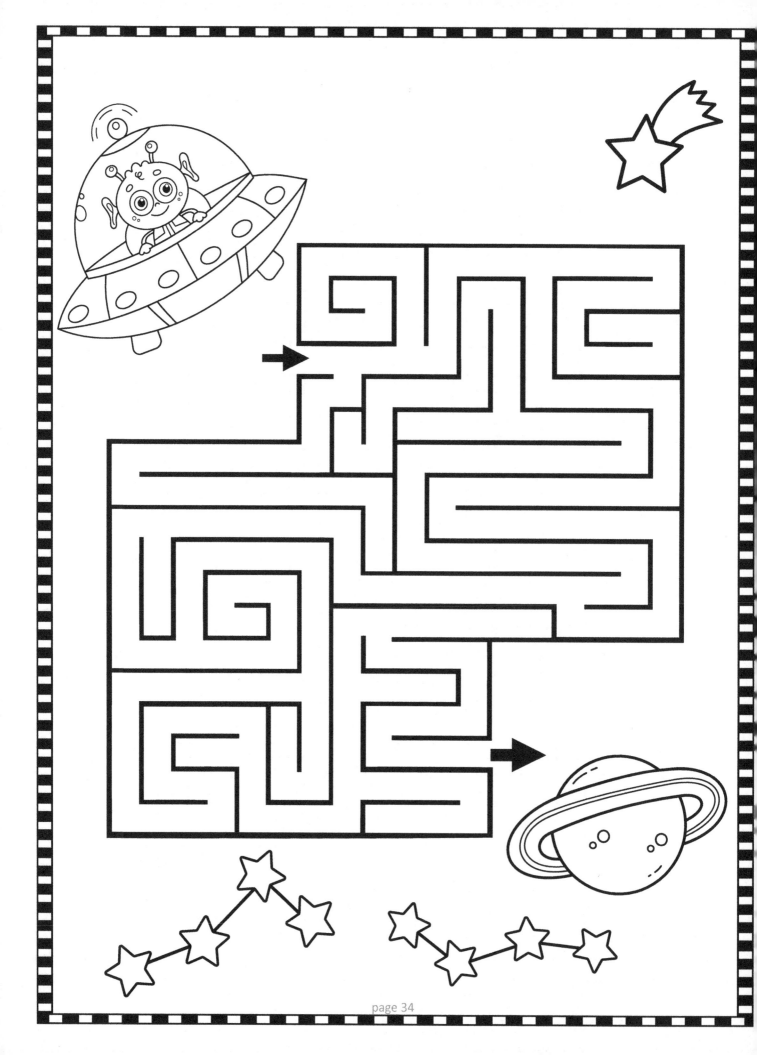

Help the friends get out of the maze

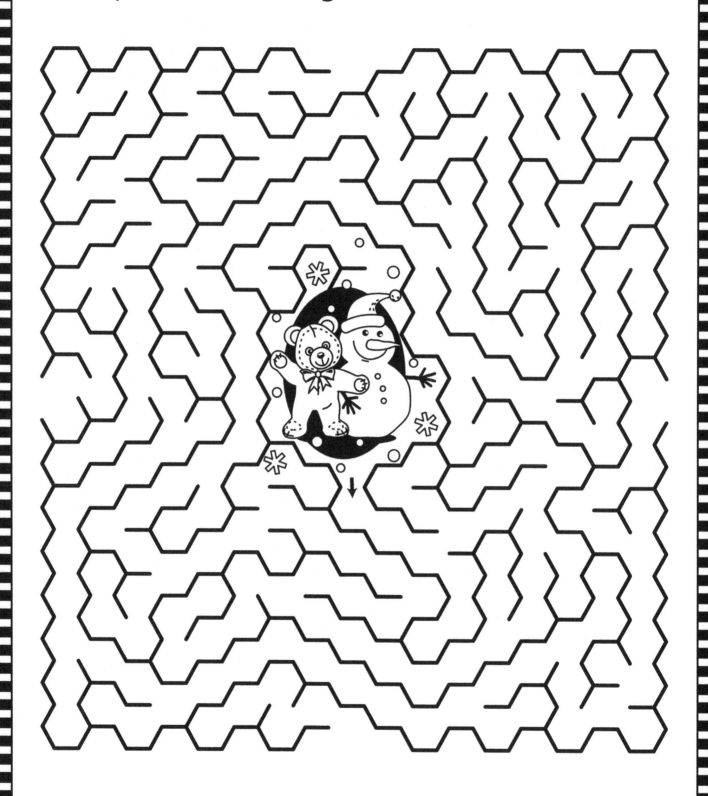

CROSSWORD

Crossword 1

Solve the puzzle and find the secret word

Crossword 2

Can you solve this puzzle?

Crossword 3

Can you solve this puzzle?

DOWN

ACROSS

Crossword 4

Can you solve this puzzle?

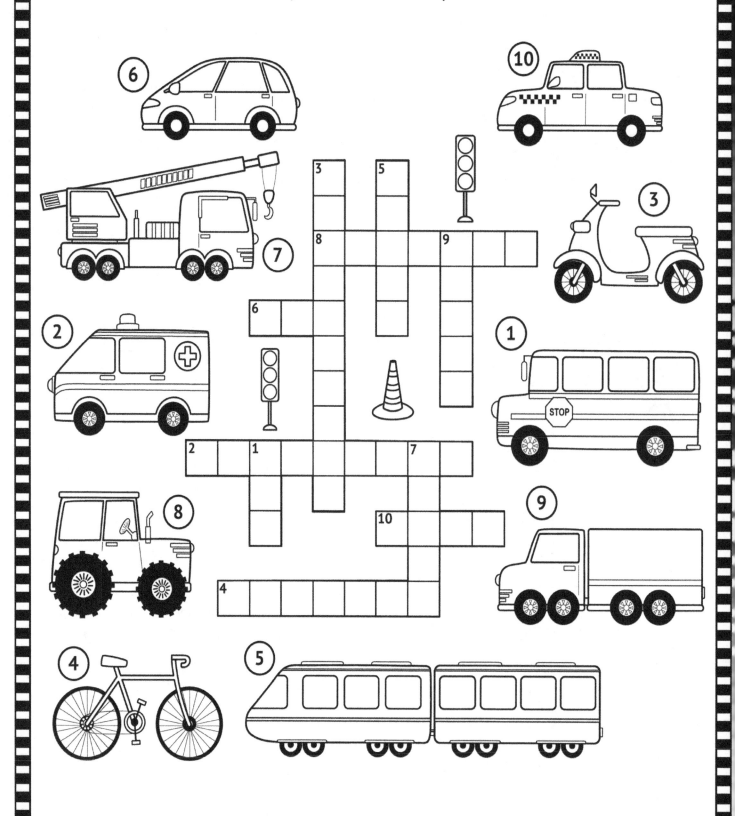

Crossword 5

Can you solve this puzzle?

Crossword 6

Can you solve this puzzle?

SPOT

THE

DIFFERENCES

Can you find 8 differences between these two pictures?

Can you find 9 differences between these two pictures?

Can you find 10 differences between these two pictures?

Can you find 10 differences between these two pictures?

Can you find 10 differences between these two pictures?

Can you find 10 differences between these two pictures?

Can you find 10 differences between these two pictures?

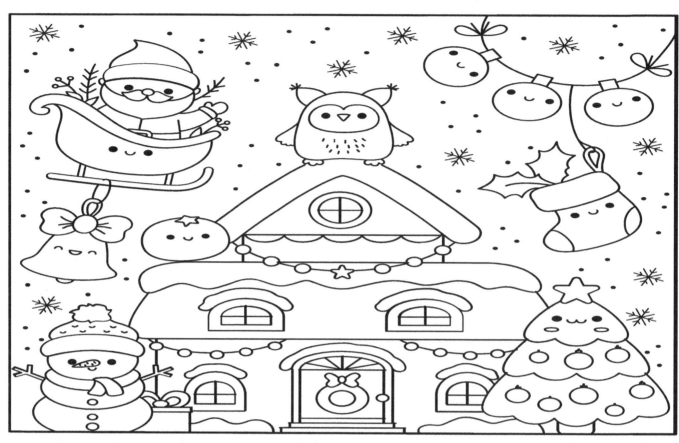

Can you find 10 differences between these two pictures?

COLORING BY NUMBERS

Dark blue 8 Yellow 6 Coral Pink 4 Grass green 1

Light brown 2 Orange 5 Sky Blue 7 Dark brown 3

Orange ▷ 1   Blue ▷ 5   Grass green ▷ 4   Dark brown ▷ 8

Yellow ▷ 7   Cherry Pick ▷ 6   Light brown ▷ 2   Light blue ▷ 3

Forest green ▷ 1   Green ▷ 3   Dark brown ▷ 4   Light brown ▷ 7

Blue ▷ 8   Sky Blue ▷ 6   Neon yellow ▷ 2   Cream ▷ 5

Light green ➤ 3   Light blue ➤ 1   Coral Pink ➤ 7   Orange ➤ 4

Grass green ➤ 2   Yellow ➤ 6   Beige ➤ 8   Red ➤ 5

Light orange > 3   Green > 1   Red > 7   Blue > 4

Dark green > 2   Gray > 6   Light blue > 8   Yellow > 5

Dark brown ⟫ 1   Blue ⟫ 6   Dark yellow ⟫ 7   Dark blue ⟫ 8

Brown ⟫ 3   Light brown ⟫ 2   Dark violet ⟫ 4   Light blue ⟫ 5

Blood red ▷ 1   Blue ▷ 6   Aqua ▷ 7

Red ▷ 3   Yellow ▷ 2   Pink ▷ 4   Green ▷ 5

page 71

DOT TO DOT

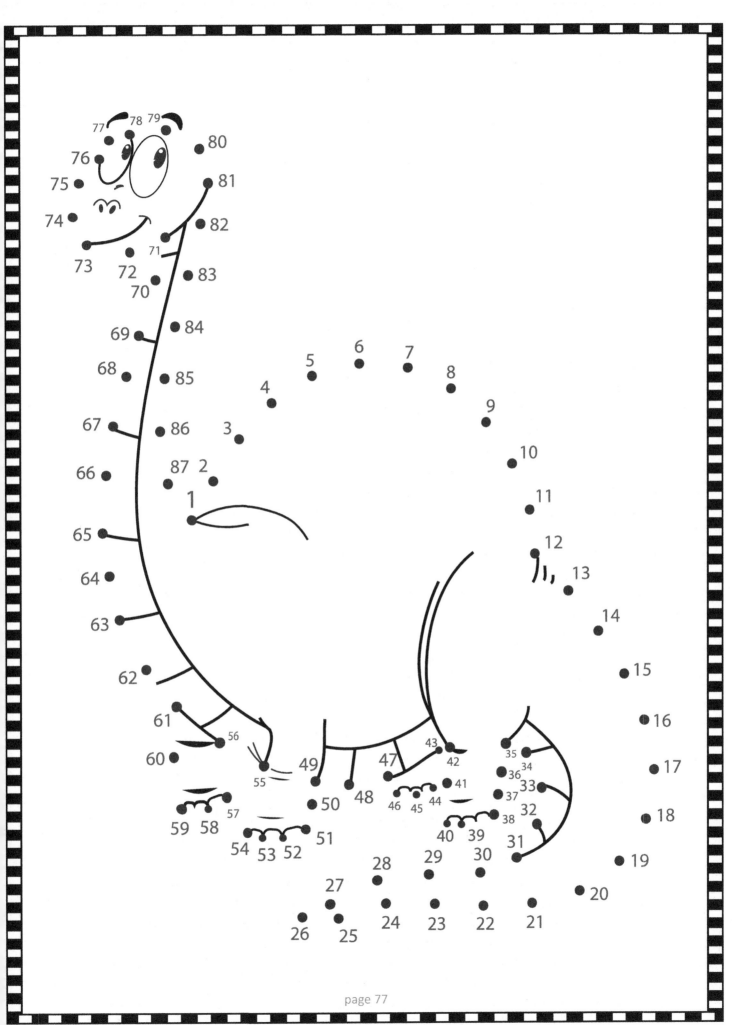

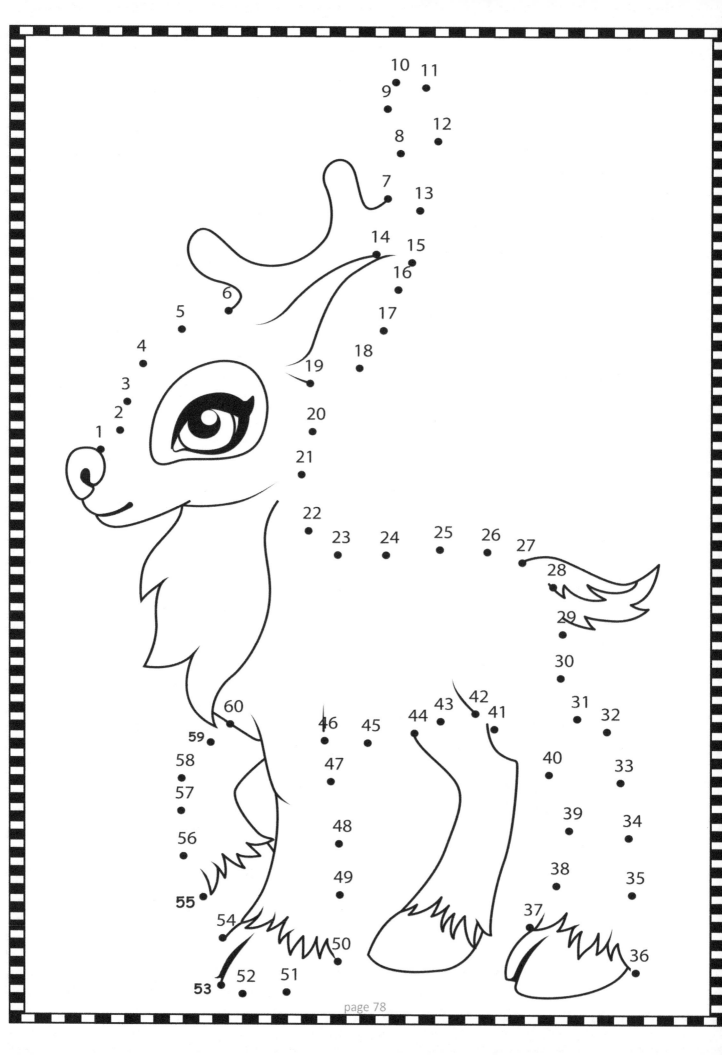

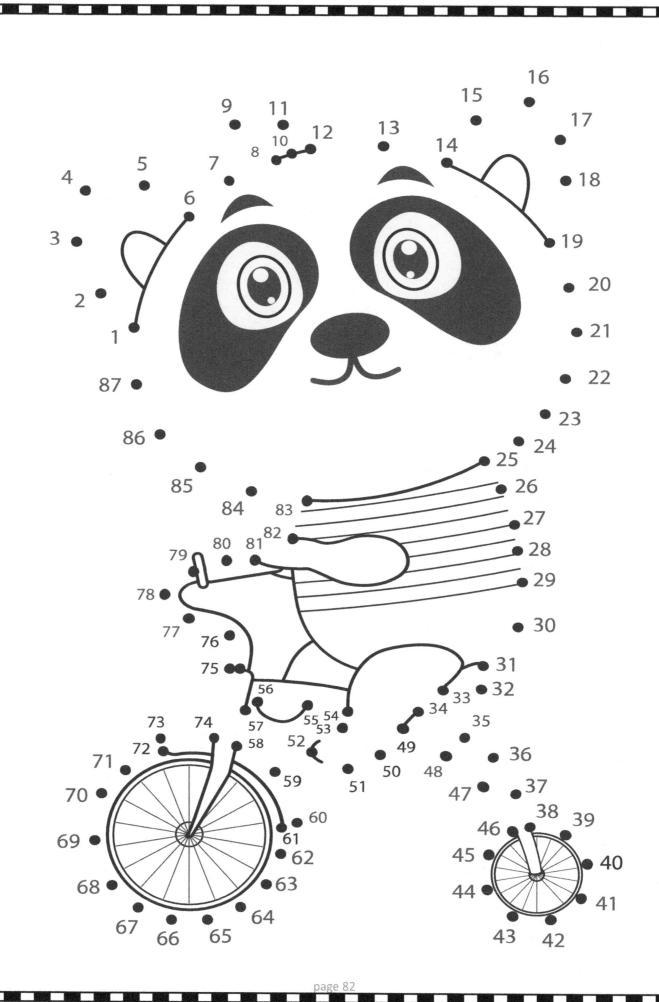

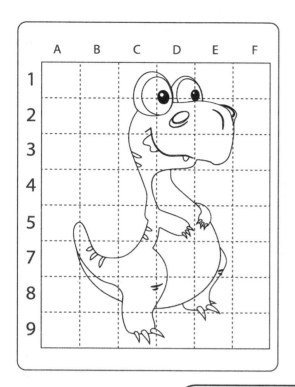

DINOSAUR

YOUR TURN

	A	B	C	D	E	F
1						
2						
3						
4						
5						
7						
8						
9						

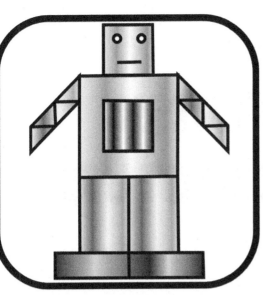

COMPLETE THE PICTURE USING GRID LINES!

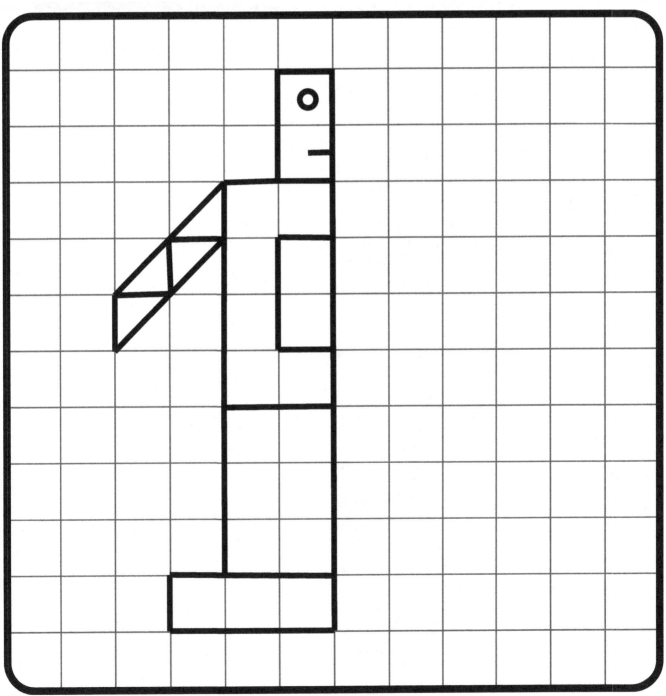

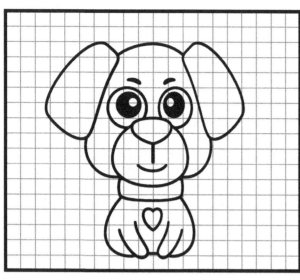

FINISH THE PICTURE

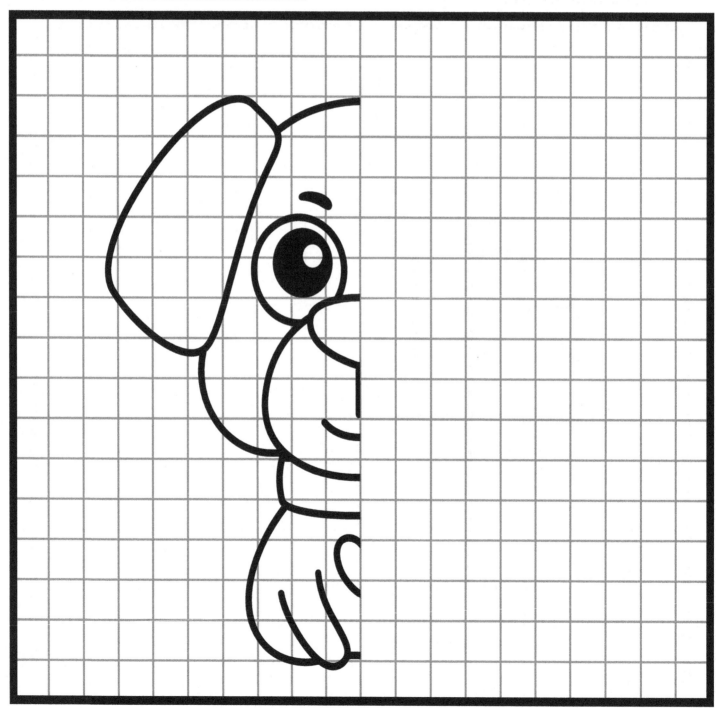

LION

YOUR TURN

	A	B	C	D	E	F
1						
2						
3						
4						
5						
7						
8						
9						

COMPLETE THE PICTURE USING GRID LINES!

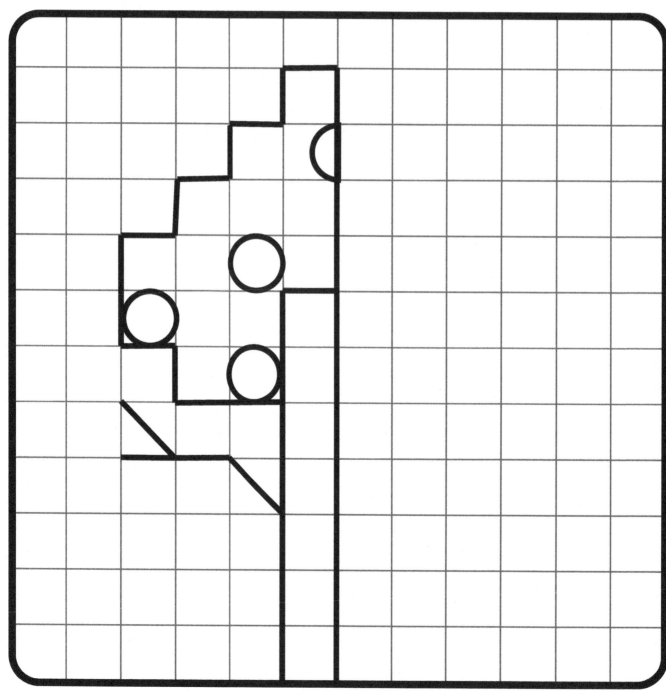

FINISH
THE PICTURE

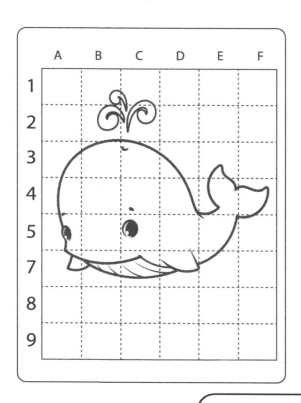

WHALE

YOUR TURN

	A	B	C	D	E	F
1						
2						
3						
4						
5						
7						
8						
9						

COMPLETE THE PICTURE USING GRID LINES!

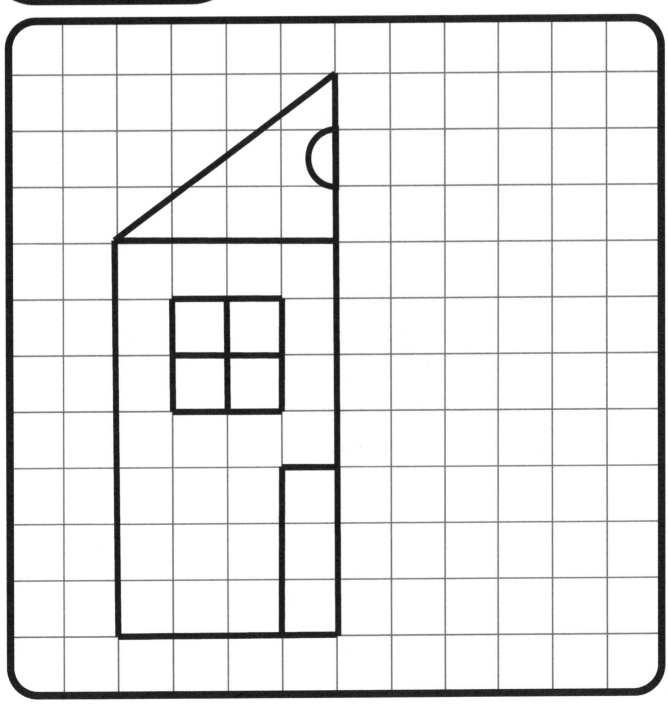

FINISH THE PICTURE

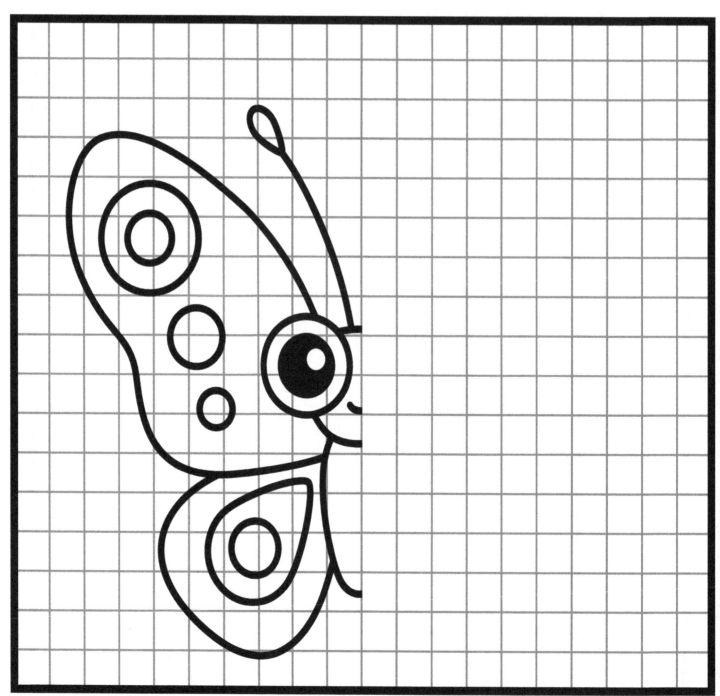

WORD SCRAMBLE

Ecological word scramble

ROLAS NELAP _____

DWIN RUTBINE _____

ROCTEEL RAC _____

PTANL _____

TENAPL _____

NERTAICON _____

REET _____

TINGROS _____

Endangered animals and plants word scramble

PARODEL _____

LEHAW _____

RETIG _____

DANAP _____

CLABK MURLE _____

RAPOL EARB _____

CHIORD _____

BABAOB _____

Pirate word scramble

TEPIAR _____

SIHP _____

SEARUTRE _____

SHECT _____

LADISN _____

TORRAP _____

CHONAR _____

APM _____

Easter word scramble

NYBUN   _____

NEH   _____

KENCHIC   _____

KETBAS   _____

GEG   _____

HESEP   _____

ARCROT   _____

WERLOF   _____

Farm animals word scramble

OWC _____

ATOG _____

GIP _____

SEHOR _____

PESHE _____

NEH _____

ITBABR _____

STEROOR _____

Magic kingdom word scramble

ETSALC   _____

RINPEC   _____

SPRISCEN   _____

ENQUE   _____

GINK   _____

WORNC   _____

NOGRAD   _____

RAGERIAC   _____

Can you guess the 9 letter words and phrases?

Count the baubles,Count the stars
And colour them.

Can you guess the 9 letter words and phrases?

Count the snowflakes , Count the clouds
And color them.

Spot the object that has no mirrored copy

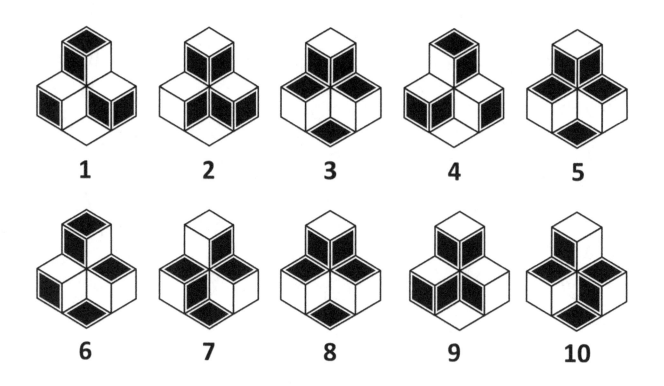

Find the unique key

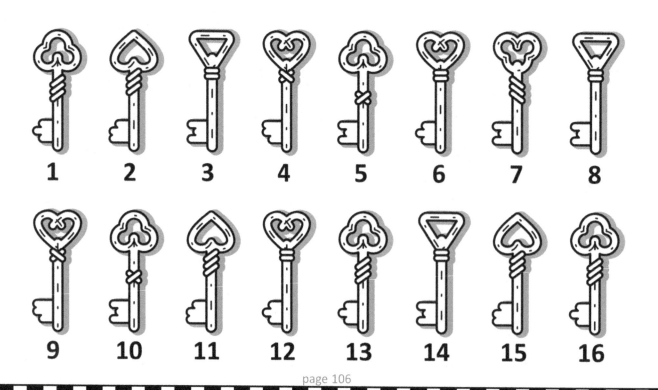

Spot the unique picture

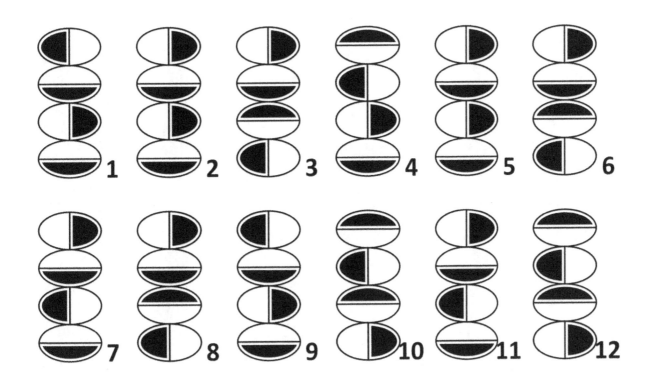

Try to find tow identical pictures

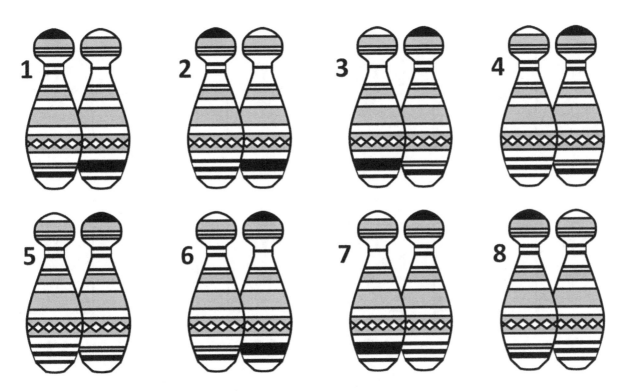

Spot the odd one out. Find the unique spoon

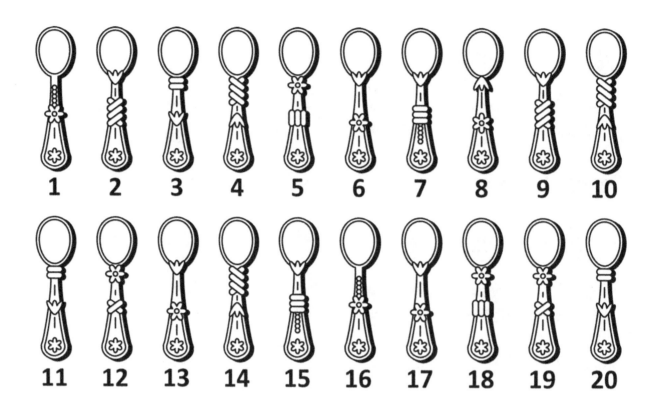

Spot the unique picture

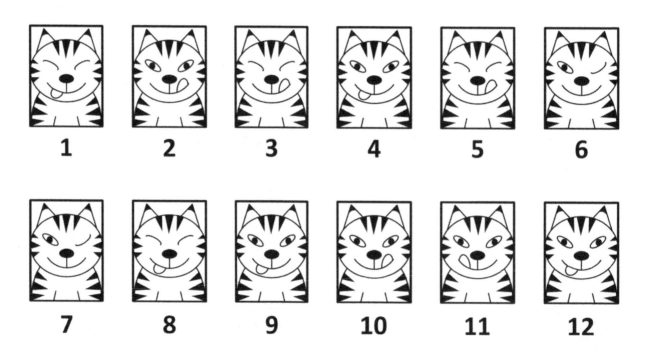

Spot the object that has no mirrored copy

Find the unique arrow

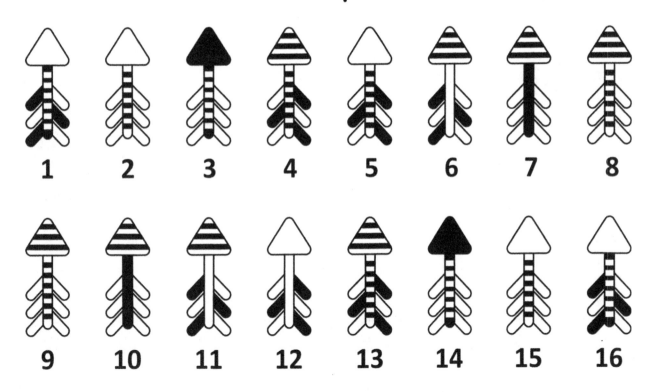

Coordinate Graphing / Draw by Coordinates

The first two coordinates are placed
as an example to solve the drawing

(10, 7), (10, 5), (11, 3), (12, 2), (11, 1), (10, 1), (9, 2), (8, 4), (7, 2), (6, 1), (5, 1), (4, 2), (5, 3), (6, 5), (6, 7), (4, 6), (3, 7), (4, 8), (6, 9), (7, 9), (6, 10), (6, 12), (7, 13), (9, 13), (10, 12), (10, 10), (9, 9), (10, 9), (12, 8), (13, 7), (12, 6), (10, 7).

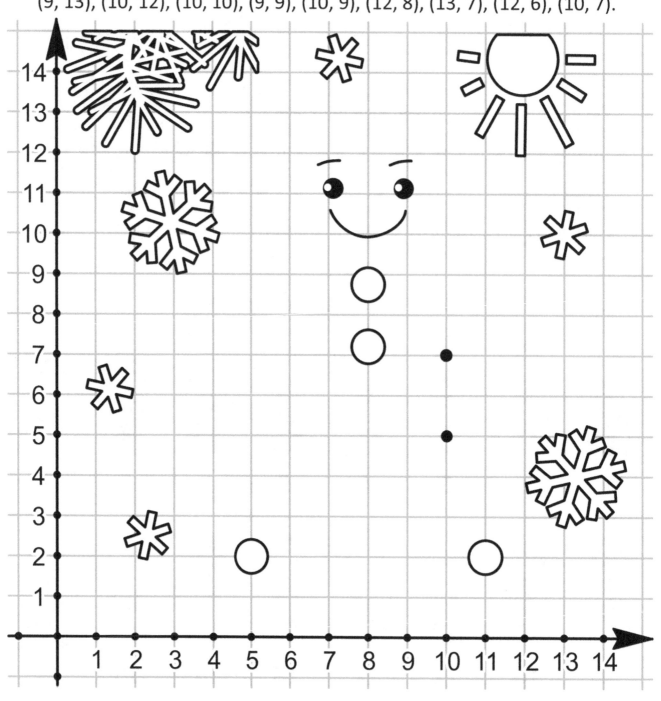

Coordinate Graphing / Draw by Coordinates

The first two coordinates are placed as an example to solve the drawing

(11, 13), (12, 12), (13, 12), (12, 11), (13, 10), (12, 10), (12, 6), (11, 4), (9, 3), (10, 2), (12, 1), (9, 1), (9, 2), (8, 3), (7, 3), (6, 2), (8, 1), (5, 1), (5, 2), (6, 3), (3, 5), (2, 7), (2, 10), (4, 9), (7, 9), (8, 10), (8, 12), (9, 13), (11, 13), (11, 14), (10, 13), (9, 14), (9, 13) and (4, 8), (5, 6), (8, 5), (9, 7).

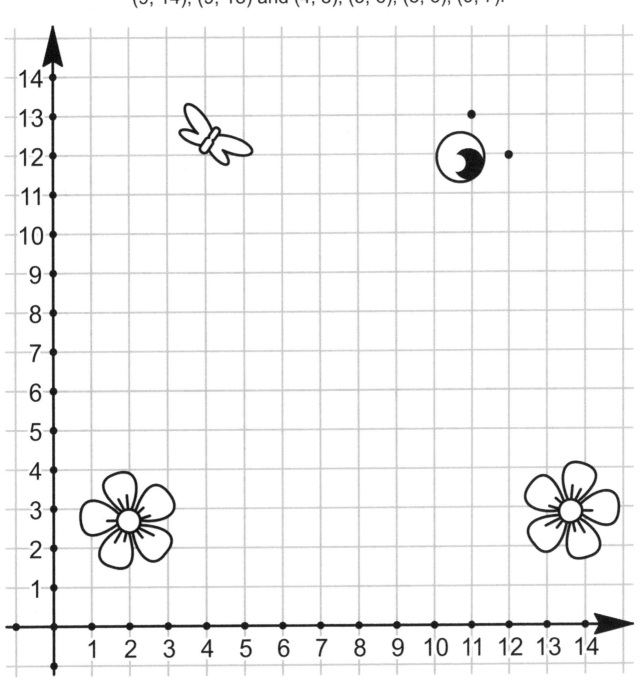

FLOWERS

This is a zigzag word search puzzle,
Words go left, right, up, and down, not diagonally,
and can bend at a right angle. There are no unused letters in the grid,
each letter is only used once.

Find all the words from the words list (ignore spaces and dashes)

C	W	E	R	A	C	B	L	U	E
O	O	R	N	A	T	L	L	E	B
R	L	L	I	P	I	O	N	D	A
N	F	U	T	A	D	R	Y	A	I
F	P	A	N	I	S	H	S	H	L
O	T	Y	S	Y	Y	C	A	N	T
R	O	E	L	L	M	U	M	E	H
G	N	E	V	A	G	L	A	D	I
E	E	H	T	F	O	S	U	L	O
T	M	L	I	L	Y	R	O	S	E

BLUEBELL	CORNFLOWER	FORGET ME NOT	PANSY
CARNATION	DAHLIA	GLADIOLUS	ROSE
CHRYSANTHEMUM	DAISY	LILY OF THE VALLEY	TULIP

AUTUMN

This is a zigzag word search puzzle,
Words go left, right, up, and down, not diagonally,
and can bend at a right angle. There are no unused letters in the grid,
each letter is only used once.

Find all the words from the words list (ignore spaces and dashes)

P	U	D	S	R	V	T	O	S	C
E	L	D	E	A	E	K	E	M	H
O	E	R	P	H	S	C	V	B	O
C	B	R	T	R	T	A	O	E	O
T	O	E	E	A	I	B	N	R	L
R	S	B	M	N	N	F	A	L	L
U	E	A	S	O	E	L	G	N	I
B	H	A	L	L	A	V	E	S	C
B	S	T	O	O	W	E	E	N	O
E	R	B	O	E	Z	A	M	N	R

BACK TO SCHOOL   **HALLOWEEN**   **OCTOBER**   **RUBBER BOOTS**

CORN MAZE   **HARVEST**   **PUDDLE**   **SEASON**

FALLING LEAVES   **NOVEMBER**   **RAIN**   **SEPTEMBER**

BEACH

This is a zigzag word search puzzle,
Words go left, right, up, and down, not diagonally,
and can bend at a right angle. There are no unused letters in the grid,
each letter is only used once.

Find all the words from the words list (ignore spaces and dashes)

S	U	N	B	A	T	L	A	O	C
C	R	G	N	I	H	L	N	A	E
B	A	U	M	B	R	E	L	A	V
M	I	W	S	A	S	S	L	B	O
M	I	N	G	N	D	E	A	Y	L
L	E	T	O	L	S	E	S	E	L
B	P	F	W	L	U	G	S	T	S
B	I	L	E	L	G	L	A	I	W
E	L	O	S	U	N	E	G	U	I
P	F	P	S	L	O	U	N	S	M

CRAB   PEBBLE   SWIMMING

FLIP-FLOPS   SAND      SWIMSUIT

GULL   SEA   TOWEL

LOUNGE   SUNBATHING   UMBRELLA

OCEAN   SUNGLASSES   VOLLEYBALL

INSECTS

This is a zigzag word search puzzle,
Words go left, right, up, and down, not diagonally,
and can bend at a right angle. There are no unused letters in the grid,
each letter is only used once.

Find all the words from the words list (ignore spaces and dashes)

L	A	D	Y	F	L	Y	B	U	M
G	G	U	B	E	E	B	E	L	B
R	R	O	W	Y	L	F	R	E	A
A	E	T	A	B	E	R	P	T	N
S	P	I	S	E	L	E	I	T	T
S	P	U	P	E	T	T	L	U	B
H	O	Q	S	P	I	A	L	B	Y
M	O	S	R	E	D	C	A	E	L
O	R	M	S	B	U	G	R	E	F
W	K	L	I	D	R	A	G	O	N

BUTTERFLY	ANT	LADYBUG
CATERPILLAR	BEE	MOSQUITO
DRAGONFLY	BEETLE	SILKWORM
FLY	BUG	SPIDER
GRASSHOPPER	BUMBLEBEE	WASP

page 115

BIRDS

This is a zigzag word search puzzle,
Words go left, right, up, and down, not diagonally,
and can bend at a right angle. There are no unused letters in the grid,
each letter is only used once.

Find all the words from the words list (ignore spaces and dashes)

P	T	C	U	C	K	O	F	L	A
A	O	S	W	A	N	O	S	E	M
R	R	K	I	A	V	E	N	A	I
H	A	C	N	R	C	K	L	G	N
E	E	O	G	D	U	S	L	U	G
R	P	C	F	R	E	W	A	O	O
O	N	K	I	S	H	R	L	W	L
R	A	N	E	D	O	E	L	O	W
C	B	U	L	L	V	K	C	E	P
H	C	N	I	F	E	W	O	O	D

BULLFINCH	DUCK	OWL	SEAGULL
CRANE	FLAMINGO	PARROT	SWALLOW
CUCKOO	HERON	PEACOCK	SWAN
DOVE	KINGFISHER	RAVEN	WOODPECKER

ZOO ANIMALS

This is a zigzag word search puzzle,
Words go left, right, up, and down, not diagonally,
and can bend at a right angle. There are no unused letters in the grid,
each letter is only used once.

Find all the words from the words list (ignore spaces and dashes)

G	I	R	Z	E	B	H	I	M	P
P	H	A	C	A	R	C	E	L	A
E	A	F	R	O	C	O	D	I	N
L	N	F	O	S	T	R	E	E	Z
E	T	E	P	H	C	I	H	O	F
K	A	H	Y	L	I	O	A	G	L
O	R	I	T	N	C	N	T	N	A
O	R	P	H	O	H	E	E	I	M
K	U	P	O	N	O	P	O	R	C
A	B	R	H	I	E	N	I	P	U

CHEETAN

CHIMPANZEE

CROCODILE

ELEPHANT

FLAMINGO

GIRAFFE

HIPPO

KOOKABURRA

LION

OSTRICH

PORCUPINE

PYTHON

RHINO

ZEBRA

SOLUTION

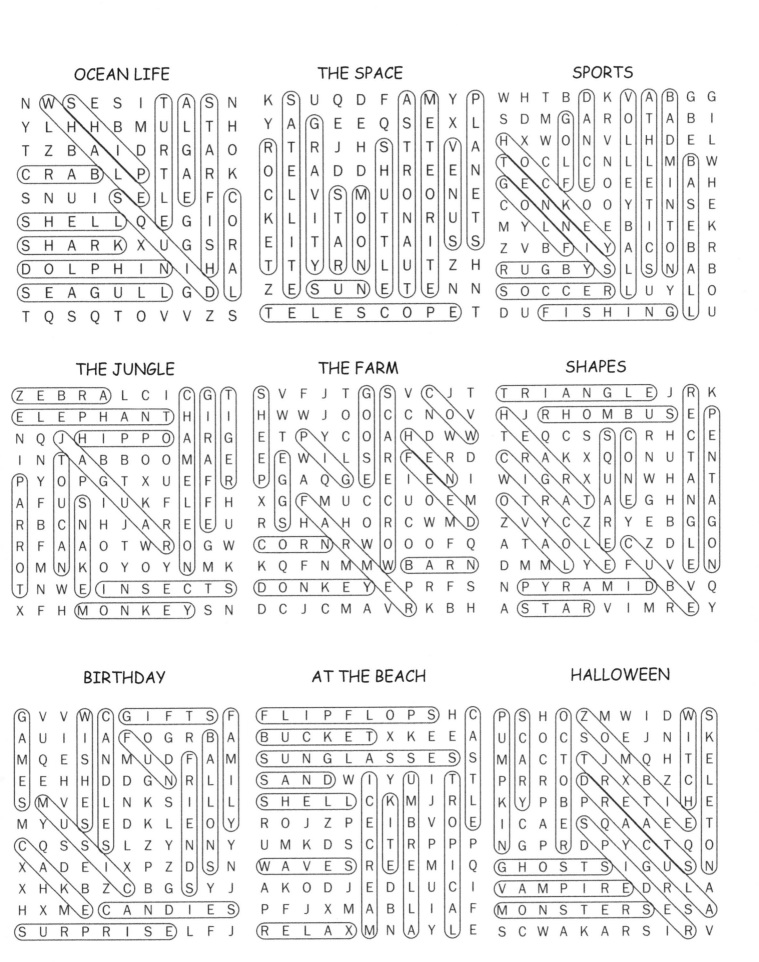

OCEAN LIFE

THE SPACE

SPORTS

THE JUNGLE

THE FARM

SHAPES

BIRTHDAY

AT THE BEACH

HALLOWEEN

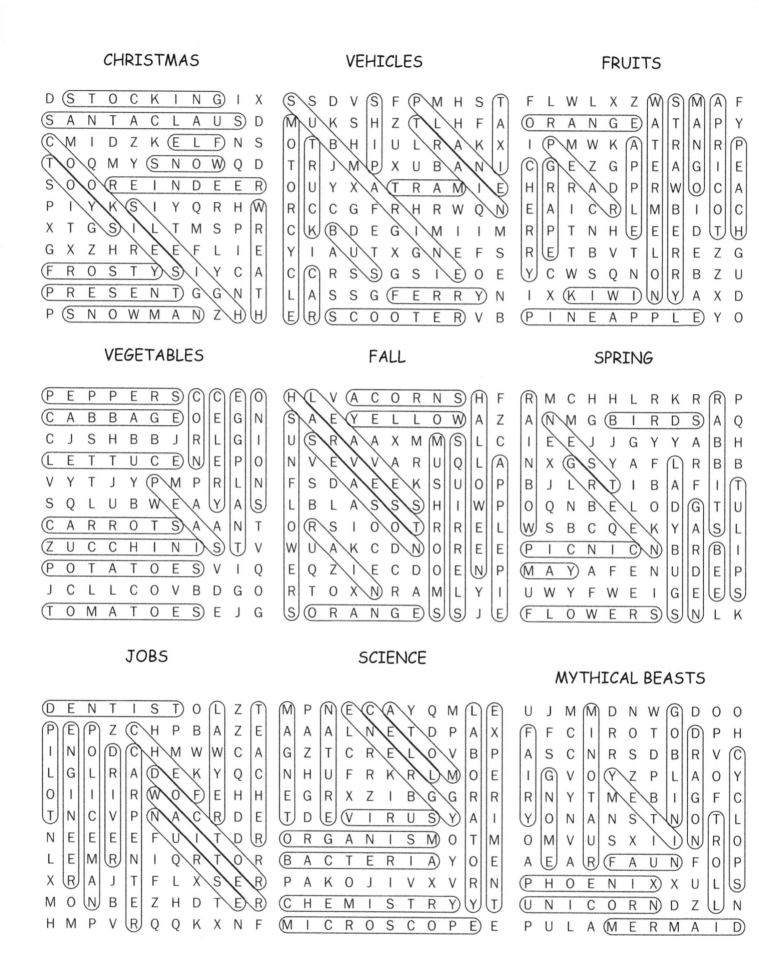

CHRISTMAS

VEHICLES

FRUITS

VEGETABLES

FALL

SPRING

JOBS

SCIENCE

MYTHICAL BEASTS

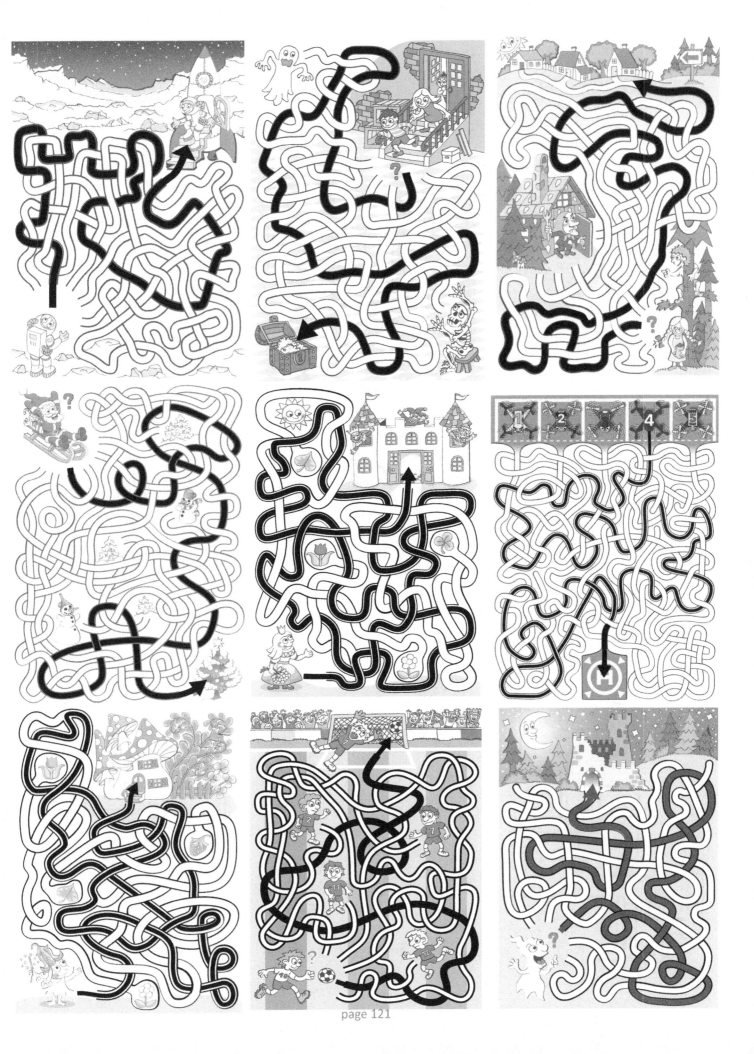

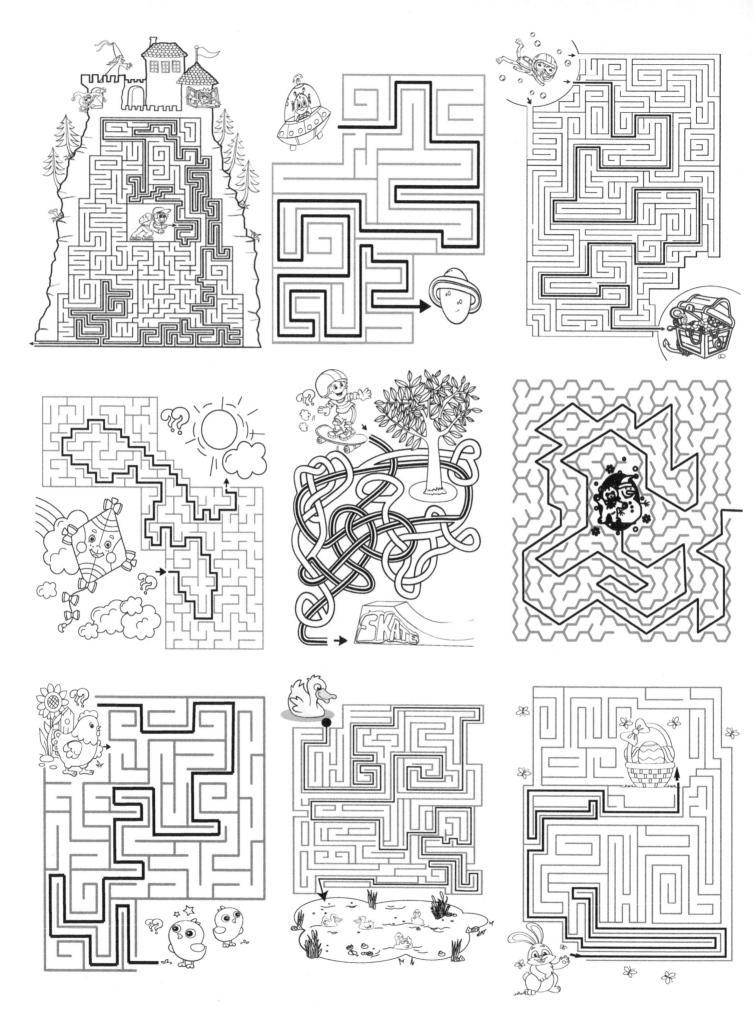

Crossword 1 solution

1. (across) bee 1. (down) butterfly 2. strawberry
3. fish 4. leaf 5. lizard 6. hive 7. flower
8. mushroom 9. (across) stone 9. (down) stump
10. ladybug 11. mouse 12. grass 13. cloud
Answer: NATURE

Crossword 2 solution

Down: 1. Poison 2. Dagger 4. Hat 5. Anchor 6. Rope 9. Hook
10. Saber 11. Rum 14. Compass 16. Flag 17. Bomb

Across: 3. Map 7. Island 8. Boot 12. Coins 13. Treasure
15. Locket 17. Barrel 18. Spyglass

Crossword 3 solution

DOWN: 1. Wisp 2. Shaver 3. Toothpaste

4. Hairdryer 5. Hairbrush 6. Shampoo

7. Bathrobe

ACROSS: 6. Spray 8. Brush 9. Mirror

10 Soap 11 Toothbrush 12 Towel

Crossword 4 solution

1.Bus 2.Ambulance
3.Motorcycle
4.Bicycle 5.Train
6.Car 7.Crane
8.Tractor 9.Truck
10.Taxi

Crossword 5 solution

1.Parrot 2.Watermelon 3.Whale
4.Bird 5.Palm 6.Airplane 7.Sunscreen
8.Cocktail 9.Skydiving 10.Sun

Crossword 6 solution

1.Grape 2.Strawberry 3.Watermelon
4.Pomegranate 5.Lemon 6.Apple 7.Pear
8.Pineapple 9.Orange 10.Banana

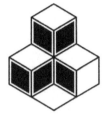

ANSWER: 9.

ANSWER: 7.

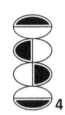

ANSWER: 4(1=9, 2=5, 3=6=8, 7=11, 10=12).

ANSWER: 4, 5.

ANSWER: 8.

ANSWER: 11.

ANSWER: 4.

ANSWER: 12.

ANSWER:

ANSWER:

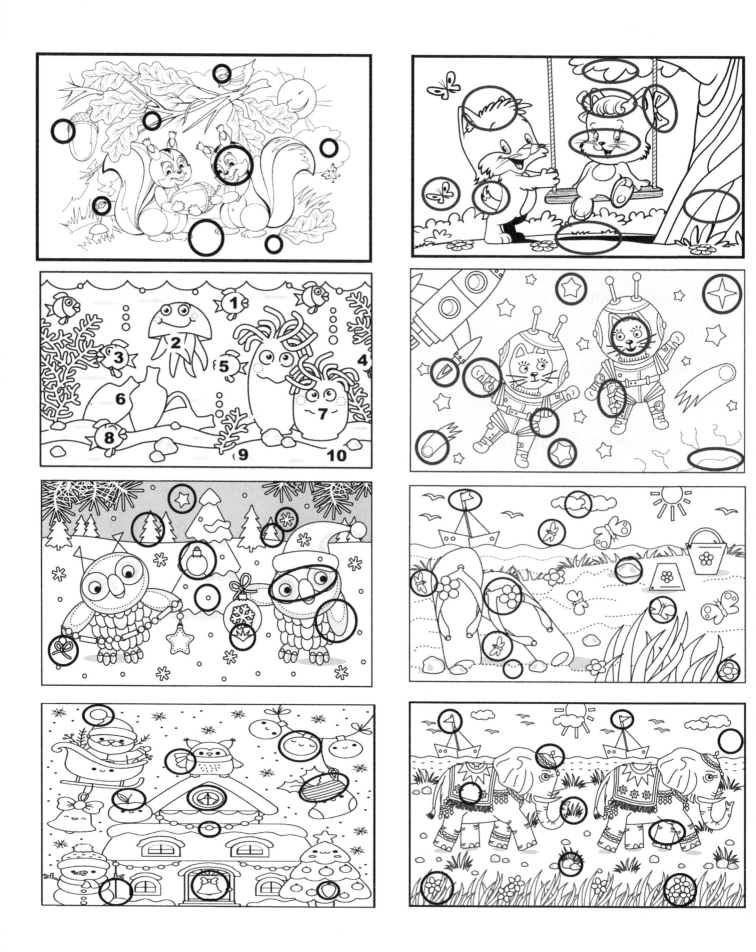

ECOLOGICAL WORD SCRAMBLE
S O L U T I O N

ROLAS NELAP — SOLAR PANEL

DWIN RUTBINE — WIND TURBINE

ROCTEEL RAC — ELECTRO CAR

PTANL — PLANT

TENAPL — PLANET

NERTAICON — CONTAINER

REET — **TREE**

TINGROS — SORTING

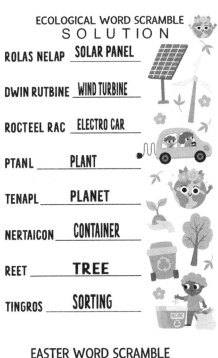

ENDANGERED ANIMALS AND PLANTS WORD SCRAMBLE
S O L U T I O N

PARODEL — LEOPARD

LEHAW — WHALE

RETIG — TIGER

DANAP — PANDA

CLABK MURLE — BLACK LEMUR

RAPOL EARB — POLAR BEAR

CHIORD — ORCHID

BABAOB — BAOBAB

PIRATE WORD SCRAMBLE
S O L U T I O N

TEPIAR — PIRATE

SIHP — SHIP

SEARUTRE — TREASURE

SHECT — CHEST

LADISN — ISLAND

TORRAP — PARROT

CHONAR — ANCHOR

APM — MAP

EASTER WORD SCRAMBLE
S O L U T I O N

NYBUN — BUNNY

NEH — HEN

KENCHIC — CHICKEN

KETBAS — BASKET

GEG — EGG

HESEP — SHEEP

ARCROT — CARROT

WERLOF — FLOWER

FARM ANIMALS WORD SCRAMBLE
S O L U T I O N

OWC — COW

ATOG — GOAT

GIP — PIG

SEHOR — HORSE

PESHE — SHEEP

NEH — HEN

ITBABR — RABBIT

STEROOR — ROOSTER

MAGIC KINGDOM WORD SCRAMBLE
S O L U T I O N

ETSALC — CASTLE

RINPEC — PRINCE

SPRISCEN — PRINCESS

ENQUE — QUEEN

GINK — KING

WORNC — CROWN

NOGRAD — DRAGON

RAGERIAC — CARRIAGE

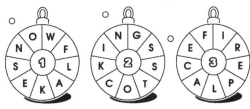

ANSWER: SNOWFLAKE, STOCKINGS, FIREPLACE, PINE CONES, CANDY CANE, NORTH POLE, MISTLETOE, BOXING DAY, GINGER MAN.

ANSWER: REINDEER, DECEMBER, BLIZZARD, HOLIDAYS, CARDINAL, ORNAMENT, SNOWFALL, GARLANDS, CARDIGAN.

baubles - 19; stars - 24.

snowflakes - 33; clouds - 20.

FLOWERS

C	W	E	R	A	C	B	L	U	E
O	O	R	N	A	T	L	L	E	B
R	L	L	I	P	I	O	N	D	A
N	F	U	T	A	D	R	Y	A	I
F	P	A	N	I	S	H	S	H	L
O	T	Y	S	Y	Y	C	A	N	T
R	O	E	L	L	M	U	M	E	H
G	N	E	V	A	G	L	A	D	I
E	E	H	T	F	O	S	U	L	O
T	M	L	I	L	Y	R	O	S	E

AUTUMN

P	U	D	S	R	V	T	O	S	C
E	L	D	E	A	E	K	E	M	H
O	E	R	P	H	S	C	V	B	O
C	B	R	T	R	T	A	O	E	O
T	O	E	E	A	I	B	N	R	L
R	S	B	M	N	N	F	A	L	L
U	E	A	S	O	E	L	G	N	I
B	H	A	L	L	A	V	E	S	C
B	S	T	O	O	W	E	E	N	O
E	R	B	O	E	Z	A	M	N	R

BEACH

S	U	N	B	A	T	L	A	O	C
C	R	G	N	I	H	L	N	A	E
B	A	U	M	B	R	E	L	A	V
M	I	W	S	A	S	S	L	B	O
M	I	N	G	N	D	E	A	Y	L
L	E	T	O	L	S	E	S	E	L
B	P	F	W	L	U	G	S	T	S
B	I	L	E	L	G	L	A	I	W
E	L	O	S	U	N	E	G	U	I
P	F	P	S	L	O	U	N	S	M

INSECTS

L	A	D	Y	F	L	Y	B	U	M
G	G	U	B	E	E	B	E	L	B
R	R	O	W	Y	L	F	R	E	A
A	E	T	A	B	E	R	P	T	N
S	P	I	S	E	L	E	I	T	T
S	P	U	P	E	T	T	L	U	B
H	O	Q	S	P	I	A	L	B	Y
M	O	S	R	E	D	C	A	E	L
O	R	M	S	B	U	G	R	E	F
W	K	L	I	D	R	A	G	O	N

BIRDS

P	T	C	U	C	K	O	F	L	A
A	O	S	W	A	N	O	S	E	M
R	R	K	I	A	V	E	N	A	I
H	A	C	N	R	C	K	L	G	N
E	E	O	G	D	U	S	L	U	G
R	P	C	F	R	E	W	A	O	O
O	N	K	I	S	H	R	L	W	L
R	A	N	E	D	O	E	L	O	W
C	B	U	L	L	V	K	C	E	P
H	C	N	I	F	E	W	O	O	D

ZOO ANIMALS

G	I	R	Z	E	B	H	I	M	P
P	H	A	C	A	R	C	E	L	A
E	A	F	R	O	C	O	D	I	N
L	N	F	O	S	T	R	E	E	Z
E	T	E	P	H	C	I	H	O	F
K	A	H	Y	L	I	O	A	G	L
O	R	I	T	N	C	N	T	N	A
O	R	P	H	O	H	E	E	I	M
K	U	P	O	N	O	P	O	R	C
A	B	R	H	I	E	N	I	P	U

THANK YOU

We are sure you had many opportunities to choose such a book. Thank you for choosing us, We are a small family business and your feedback is very important to us.

If you liked our book please leave us a comment at the following email address or a review on Amazon.com

 tommymcrain@gmail.com

Visit the link below, or scan the QR code to receive a 60-page gift book!

https://bit.ly/3w1zj3sTommyMcRain

 **GET YOUR GIFT BOOK NOW !** *scan me*

Made in United States
Orlando, FL
27 May 2023